SPEAK TO THE KING

MINISTER TO THE *BOY*

Relationship Drs' Tim & Monique Johns

Speak to the King, Minister to the Boy

By The Relationship Drs. Drs. Timothy & Monique Johns

Cover Designed by Louisa P. Handy

Published by Jazzy Kitty Publications

Editor: Anelda L. Attaway

© 2023 Timothy Johns

ISBN 978-1-954425-80-4

DEDICATION

I would like to dedicate "Speak to the King and Minister to the Boy" to my loving mother Theresa Johns. Her life has been an inspiration to me as a little boy and still is my motivation for me to continue growing into the King God wants me to be. Her confidence in me helped me recognize the Cheerleader I needed to marry.

To my wife Monique, thank you for taking over where my mother left off. Your strength and your vision continue to help me see like a King.

Love Tim

Mother Theresa, thank you for sacrificing your life to raise a King. I know at times it's frustrating, but your diligence and tenacity to not allow the environment to dictate Tim's movement in life. It takes not just a strong woman but a smart and strategic woman to see what your little boy needed and nurture him to his set place without hesitation. Thank you for allowing me to pick up where you left off and being there when the boy nature rises. You are not just a mother to your own but a mother to all MEN that are in search of one. Continued Blessings on your life.

Love Monique!

ACKNOWLEDGMENTS

Mom & Dad

You've been more than just mentors for Monique and me. Their presence in our lives has had a direct impact on the success we've experienced in our marriage and family.

We Love & Appreciate you.

TABLE OF CONTENTS

INTRODUCTION

All failure can be traced back to a lack of honor. What we don't honor, we will disvalue. For relationships to succeed, there have to be rules of engagement. These rules will help establish boundaries. This book was written to provide tools and strategies that we believe are necessary to make an impact on your relationship.

There are roles we all must play if we are going to see the vision for our relationships come to pass. We believe in transparency, so we have shared some of our triumphs and failures. In addition, we've gleaned strategies and principles from successful couples we've had the pleasure to meet over the years. We all come into relationships with a plurality of all types of baggage. Our cultural background, personality differences, trauma from past relationships, and outside influences create numerous challenges and untrue realities.

To win at the relationship game, you must be willing to make sacrifices and seek out or develop a strategy that will yield the results you want. You must remember that human behavior is very consistent. Discovering the personality types, tendencies, and proclivities will be necessary for you to develop a strategy to win.

Take some time for self-reflection and restart your hard drive and begin again. This is a battle that you can win, but you must unplug your emotions and get a fresh perspective. Often we can have the best strategy, but we lack the commitment, consistency, and transparency to follow through. This lack of dedication will show up when we get frustrated with not seeing results. Know for certain that change takes place in the unseen realm before you ever see it in the physical realm.

Take a moment to pray and ask the Holy Spirit to give you a divine strategy for your relationship. As you read one chapter at a time, pause, meditate, and write down what you hear. Let's take this journey together and get to work. Please don't forget to take notes on what you learned and what you will be implanting new on your journey.

CHAPTER 1

In Every Boy, There Is a Hidden King

Ladies, every man, whether he believes it or not, is born a King. As believers, we all have been given the DNA of our Heavenly Father. Whoever fathers us transfers their DNA into us at conception. We see this in the book of Genesis Chapter 2, we see God the Father breathing His DNA into our Father Adam. Adam was the first King on this planet, and this King was given this planet to rule and reign. We begin with this story because if you don't know this story, you won't be able to help him recognize who he is. Until a man knows who he is, he will never be able to bring you to a place of personal fulfillment in your relationship.

In this chapter, we will share with you how you can help your man realize he is a King. Every man who doesn't know who they are will act like a boy. Don't be fooled by a man who acts King like sometimes, but under pressure, the boy comes out. This is a sign that your man has an identity crisis. Unfortunately, many women marry boys who they thought were Kings and it is not until you begin to do life together that you realize something is wrong.

If you married this individual, don't think for one second that God made a mistake. Especially if you said that God brought you two together. Monique and I wrote this book so you would understand how to help your man step into the position of a King. God had a way of uniting two individuals with different gifts to complement one another. These differences are designed by God to bring unity.

'But our bodies have many parts, and God has put each part just where He wants it. How strange a body would be if it had only one part! Yes, there are many parts, but only one body.'

1 Corinthians 12:18-20

Don't allow what you don't like about your man to hinder the unity that is necessary for you both to have dominion. God gave Adam and Eve both dominions. Dominion can only be accomplished through unification.

We want to encourage you not to quit your relationship. You may feel that you are outgrowing him spiritually. You feel like you just can't take it anymore. Before you quit, read the rest of this book. Women of God, you play a major role in helping your man realize he is a King. Remember, this man is the product of your intelligent choice. We want you to think about this. If this man was such a bad choice, what does your decision to be with him say about you? Ladies, allow us to share something with you that I have experienced.

I have been married to my wife for 27 years and we have four beautiful children. From the outside, everything looks great, but on the inside, we are two individuals who are still learning how to love and honor one another unconditionally. God had a way of using our imperfections to perfect one another. Often, we make permanent decisions from a place of immaturity. It is our immaturity that has us preoccupied with the other person's flaws.

Now for the rest of this chapter, I want to share with you how to help your man realize he is a King. You must help him overcome his insecurities. It is our insecurities that have their roots in our fears and wherever you find fear, there is a lack of understanding. Ladies, whenever a man doesn't understand something, it is a sign that he lacks understanding. We are all afraid of the unknown. This is why most men are stagnant, idle, or simply lack momentum in their life. Your assignment is to help him overcome his fears. You must remember there is a King under that boy's exterior.

Allow me to give you an example. When I married Monique, I told my mother that this woman is a bigger fan of mine than you. Monique made me feel like I could do anything. My mother was heartbroken but never told me until years later. Deep down, she was happy that a found a wife that would encourage me to do great things. Growing up without a father in the house made me an insecure little boy. My mother had the insight and the wisdom to speak to the King and minister to the boy. She knew there was a King inside this little boy. Looking back on my relationship with my wife, I believe her belief in me motivated me to believe I could accomplish anything.

When we purchased our first house, Monique wanted a deck on the back of the house. We received several quotes and all of them were over 5,000 dollars. At that time, that was a lot of money for me. I told her that we were not spending that kind of money on a deck. Gabriella, our first daughter's birthday, was coming up in three months and she still had her heart set on the deck. My heart really wanted to get that deck for her, but we really couldn't afford it. So, one day she looked at me with those big eyes and said, "Tim, you can build the deck yourself." I said to her, "I've never built anything in my life, and you want me to build a 38X14-foot deck?"

She told me to just talk to the man at Lowes (Glenn); unbeknownst to me, she was talking to him about this deck and guided me through building it myself. She was right, Glenn at Lowes gave me a video to watch. I must have watched that video about 20 times until my confidence level grew to the point that I moved into action. Ladies, your man has the capacity of a King. It may be hidden, but it is in there. Every man needs his woman to believe in him. When the boy is talking, ignore him and speak to the King. If you speak to the King, the boy will stop talking.

The other thing you must do is put your man around a strong man who will confirm what you are saying. When my wife took me to meet Glenn at Lowes, Glenn said, "Tim, you can do this." Watching that video and having another man speak into my life was a game-changer. Hear me clearly, every man is born a King. It may be hidden behind the boy, but it is in there. You must help us dig it out.

"Where is He who has been born King of the Jews?"
Matthew 2:2

THE GAME PLAN

Reflections from this Chapter

_____

_____

_____

_____

_____

_____

_____

_____

_____

What did you learn?

➤ _____

_____

➤ _____

_____

➤ _____

_____

➤ _____

_____

What strategy do you need to implement?

➤ _____

_____

➤ _____

_____

➤ _____

_____

➤ _____

_____

What behavioral change do you need to make?

➤ _____

_____

➤ _____

_____

➤ _____

_____

➤ _____

_____

Who do you know that has perfected the behavioral change that you need to make?

➢ _____

_____

➢ _____

_____

➢ _____

_____

➢ _____

_____

Develop a strategy to perfect the behavioral change.

➢ _____

_____

➢ _____

_____

➢ _____

_____

➢ _____

_____

How will you prioritize the behavioral change?

- ➢ _____
  _____
- ➢ _____
  _____
- ➢ _____
  _____
- ➢ _____
  _____

How often will you practice it?

How will you be consistent until you perfect the change?

_____
_____
_____
_____
_____
_____
_____

CHAPTER 2

Motivated by Compassion

While Jesus walked on this earth, He was motivated by compassion. Compassion is a response of the heart. You must understand that both the King and the boy will need compassion. A simple examination of how Jesus flowed with compassion will give you all the evidence you need to walk as He did.

'But whoever keeps His word, truly the love of God is perfected in him. By this, we know that we are in Him. He who says he abides in Him ought himself also to walk just as He walked.'
I John 2:5-6

The above scripture explains that compassion flows out of the love of God. Woman of God, all that is saved has received the love of God, but that love isn't perfected (complete) until it touches someone else life. In other words, our love is immature unless we have given that love to our neighbor. Based on this scripture, we can walk as Jesus did. You must believe and understand that within you is the capacity to be everything that your relationship needs. Both the boy and the King need compassion. You must be sensitive to the Holy Spirit's promptings concerning your man. God has placed you in a position to provide what is necessary to make your man whole.

Just think about this for a moment. Jesus fed the five thousand and four thousand people with compassion. It is said in the scriptures that He was moved with compassion and healed them all. The supernatural lifestyle is manifested through a man or woman who has compassion. The cross of Christ is an example of God's compassion. Compassion is your response to the needs of your man. If you are going to flow with a compassionate heart, you must change how you see things. God has given you the ability to see the end from the beginning, which will motivate your compassion.

Jesus looked at our situation and knew that if He didn't go to the cross and surrender His life, the world would be lost forever. What He saw motivated Him to give His life. When it comes to our relationships, we see like Jesus. It is not until we understand that if we don't do what is necessary, the person we love will not make it. This should be our motivation. Jesus himself said, "that it was for the joy that was set before him that he endured the cross (Heb 12:2)." Often, showing compassion requires a dying to self. He must remember that in you is the capacity to provide whatever is necessary. You simply must be willing to provide it.

The King will need your compassion when he makes mistakes. The worst thing that can happen to a King is when a King stops taking territory. A King who stops taking territory is a King who stops taking risks. Men who are afraid of failure will not take risks. Kings are made to rule and reign. We are called to advance the kingdom initiative. To do that, we must continue to move by faith and not by sight. Mistakes are a part of our development. The King must believe that you are with him 100% and that he is free to fail if necessary.

I want to bring your attention to the picture in the scriptures: Abraham and Sarah. Abraham had sexual relations with his second wife, Hagar. Hagar became pregnant with Ishmael. The scriptures tell us that Ishmael is the son of a bondwoman. Once Abraham and Sarah realized this was a mistake, they had to continue to believe in God for the promised seed of Abraham.

The point I'm making here is that once a mistake is made, there still must be movement toward God's original intent. The King must try again, and you play a significant role in his mental fortitude.

'The godly may trip seven times, but they will get up again. But one disaster is enough to overthrow the wicked.'
Proverbs 24:16

Just because we make mistakes, we don't stop being Kings.

A King needs to be reminded that mistakes don't determine identity; they validate our identity.

Your compassion for the boy King would be a little different. Remember, inside, every boy is a King. You must remember that the boy and the King are the same person. The manifestation of the boy is an indication that the mind has slipped back into a default position. Allow me to explain. When a man is learning how to receive his new identity in Christ, he will slip back into the boy mentality under pressure. When this occurs, it's so critical that he's handled with special care. A good illustration is how a mother handles her boy, who will soon become a man. A mother is very sensitive and deliberate about how she handles the boy. Her main goal is nurturing her boy to become a man.

'He will not crush the weakest reed or put out a flickering candle. He will bring justice to all who have been wronged.'
Isaiah 42:3

The above scriptures give us the necessary imagery for us to see why we must handle the boys (flickering fame) with care. Everyone knows that the flickering candle came to be blown out by a sudden movement of air in the room. Your voice is the air in the room; what and how you say it is critical. You must remember that the same flickering candle (Boy) can become an inferno (King).

'Knowledge puffs up, but love edifies.'
I Corinthians 8:1

'but, speaking the truth in love, may grow up in all things into Him who is the head—Christ—'
Ephesians 4:15

As a woman who loves a man, must approach this as an assignment. You are graced to be a mother to a boy and a Queen to the King. Little boys need their mothers because they know that despite their internal struggles' moms will always love them. A mother's love is not motivated by the boy's performance. A mother's words will always edify, even when correcting her boy. Speaking the truth in love simply means that your words are given with the motivation of growth. In other words, you want to see your man mature.

To be motivated by compassion, you must see the end from the beginning. When God looks at us in our immature state, it's His compassion for us that motivates His action to meet our every need. In relationships, we must be able to see the end from the beginning.

Spend some time with the Holy Spirit and ask for the strategic role you play in helping the boy become a King. This role will require courage. You must not allow fear to stop you from speaking the truth in love. Many relationships fail because they are living in fear of one another. Truth spoken in love is absent of fear. Remember, it's the truth that brings freedom and fear produces bondage. Make a decision today not to allow fear to exist in your relationships.

'And when Jesus went out He saw a great multitude, and He was moved with compassion for them, and healed their sick.'

Matthew 14:14

THE GAME PLAN

Reflections from this Chapter

_____

_____

_____

_____

_____

_____

_____

_____

What did you learn?

➢ _____

_____

➢ _____

_____

➢ _____

_____

➢ _____

_____

What strategy do you need to implement?

- ➢ _____
  _____

- ➢ _____
  _____

- ➢ _____
  _____

- ➢ _____
  _____

What behavioral change do you need to make?

- ➢ _____
  _____

- ➢ _____
  _____

- ➢ _____
  _____

- ➢ _____
  _____

Who do you know that has perfected the behavioral change that you need to make?

➢ _____

➢ _____

➢ _____

➢ _____

Develop a strategy to perfect the behavioral change.

➢ _____

➢ _____

➢ _____

➢ _____

How will you prioritize the behavioral change?

➢ _____

_____

➢ _____

_____

➢ _____

_____

➢ _____

_____

How often will you practice it?

How will you be consistent until you perfect the change?

_____

_____

_____

_____

_____

_____

_____

CHAPTER 3

Discovering Your Assignment

In every successful relationship, some roles must be clearly defined. Look at some of the famous couples we know by name: Denzell & Paulette Washington, Bishop TD & Serita Jakes, and Barak & Michelle Obama. Just for fun, think of some of the most successful couples you know. What do they have in common? I would submit to you that they have discovered their assignment to one another.

The success and failure of your relationship will be primarily connected to your discovering your assignment. During a long ride to the Pocono Mountains, we received some very good advice from one of my dear friends. She looked at me and said, "Tim, you must discover your assignment, develop your assignment, and deliver your assignment." Those three phrases have never left my heart. In every relationship this assignment, you must discover. You can't stop at discovery; you must develop it. And you can't stop at development, you must deliver it.

Take a quick look at the human body. Every body part of the human body has an assignment. If the hands and eyes cannot fulfill their assignment to the body, the body is labeled as handicapped. You and I must remember that once we get into a relationship, our number one objective is to discover your assignment. Without the discovery of the assignment, there will be no fulfillment or a sense of purpose.

There is a phase we use in business that we would like to introduce to you. This phase is called a SWOT analysis. Let's conduct your own

SWOT analysis. This tool will be very helpful in you discovering your assignment. Answer the following questions:

What do you believe your strengths are in the relationship?

> What is your value to the relationship?

> What can you provide that the relationship can't survive without?

What are your weaknesses?

> Your weaknesses help you identify what you need from the other person.

What are the opportunities?

> Look for moments to provide what is necessary.

> Challenges must be looked at as opportunities Identify the Threats.

> Refusing to embrace the other person's differences.

> Refusing to die to self.

> Not understanding that differences create opportunities to unify.

I believe that every successful relationship is successful because the participants in that relationship have discovered their roles, assignment, and authority to one another. There is an unwritten law that opposites attract. Opposites attract because we have an innate desire to have the gaps in our lives filled by our relationships.

Therefore, it is dangerous to be in a relationship and not know who you are. Because if you don't know who you are, you won't know your value or self-worth. To be a gap filler in someone else life, you must know where you fit. Otherwise, you find yourself becoming what they want instead of who you need to become. Take a moment and look at Barak and Michelle Obama. I don't know them personally, but it appears Michelle knows who she is and she discovered a long time ago what role she needed to play in Barak's life. I will spend more time on this subject in a later chapter, but I thought it was necessary to introduce it now as we discuss the SWOT analysis.

There is one other point I want to highlight as we close this chapter and that is embracing the other person's differences. The violation of this principle may be the number source of relationship failures. You may have to accept some things you don't like to receive what you really need. In other words, what you love about a person, maybe the same thing that you hate. Don't allow what you hate to have you reject what is necessary. And don't allow what you hate to stop you from giving what is necessary.

Embracing the other person's differences is simply getting in agreement with them. The agreement maintained is called UNITY. The reason the human body is a masterpiece of God is that every body part knows its role and assignment. By embracing our differences, we promote unity.

'And I will pray for the Father, and He will give you another Helper, that He may abide with you forever—'
John 14:16

THE GAME PLAN

Reflections from this Chapter

_____

_____

_____

_____

_____

_____

_____

_____

What did you learn?

➤ _____

_____

➤ _____

_____

➤ _____

_____

➤ _____

_____

What strategy do you need to implement?

➢ _____

_____

➢ _____

_____

➢ _____

_____

➢ _____

_____

What behavioral change do you need to make?

➢ _____

_____

➢ _____

_____

➢ _____

_____

➢ _____

_____

Who do you know that has perfected the behavioral change that you need to make?

➢ _____

_____

➢ _____

_____

➢ _____

_____

➢ _____

_____

Develop a strategy to perfect the behavioral change.

➢ _____

_____

➢ _____

_____

➢ _____

_____

➢ _____

_____

How will you prioritize the behavioral change?

➢ _____

_____

➢ _____

_____

➢ _____

_____

➢ _____

_____

How often will you practice it?

How will you be consistent until you perfect the change?

_____

_____

_____

_____

_____

_____

_____

CHAPTER 4

Healing the Boys 'Wounds

Every human being was born with cracks in their foundation. These cracks in our foundation begin to materialize when we get into relationships. This is the same reason why this planet will always have earthquakes. Earthquakes occur when two pieces of earth plates separate under the pressure of maintaining a connection. The gap between these two earth plates is called fault lines or cracks. It is the pressure that is placed on the cracks in our foundation that reveals our wounds.

Remember what we said in an earlier chapter, "The boy and King are the same people." To heal the wounds of the boy, you must first recognize the behavior of the King under pressure. It is how he will handle the pressures of life that reveals his belief system or his strongholds. As human individuals, we can have good and bad strongholds. Most strongholds aren't built overnight, they are built over years. It is imperative that if you are going to Speak to the King; and Minister to the boy, you must study their behavior patterns.

Allow me to give you an example. Every one of us will encounter the Spirit of Rejection during our lifetime. The symptoms of the root of rejection can be the following: Aggressive reactions, Refusal to be consoled, Rejection of others, Emotional hardness, Doubt and Disbelief, Aggressive attitude, Argumentative, Rebellious, and Fights. Often these symptoms show when we experience the pressures of life.

Earlier in our marriage, I was the type of person that was easily offended. Whenever my wife challenged my thoughts or my way of thinking, I would get really defensive and sometimes irritated. One evening she planned to have a conversation with me and she needed me to hear her without offense. Before she said a word, she touched my hands and looked me straight in the eyes. She preceded to say that she loved me, and she was about to say something that I wouldn't like. The cause of my being easily offended had its roots in the Spirit of Rejection.

The wounds of the soul must be healed if you are going to live a victorious life. The above scripture speaks to the truth that the prosperity of the soul is dependent upon the soul being healed. We can only prosper to the degree that our soul prospers. The soul is like a container and every container has a capacity. As the soul is healed from the wounds from our childhood, relationships, traumatic events, and the spirit of rejection, we grow and mature. As my wife touched my hand and said those words to me, "I love you," the King in me allowed her to minister to the boy.

To heal the wounds in the boy, the King must give you access to the boy.

Every man has fears. The problem with most men is that we are uncomfortable becoming that vulnerable with the woman we love. I will guarantee you that if you locate the King's fears, you will locate the boy. Fear, at its very root, is the source of all dysfunctional behavior. Fear is the root cause of the following in most men.

> ➢ Pride – living without God
> ➢ Timidity – resist being pushed to higher levels

➢ Lack of Accountability – refusal to submit to another man

➢ Controlling – insecurities

➢ Anger – argumentative

We want to encourage you to write down what you believe is the major challenge you are having with your husband, man, son, or friend. Now pray this prayer with me at loud.

Father, in the Name of Jesus, enlighten the eyes of my understanding and give me a decerning spirit that I may have an encounter with Your truth that will set my (husband, son, or friend, man) free in the Name of Jesus. Give me the words to say that are seasoned with salt and grace that will break through all strongholds that are rooted in fear. Now, Father, I thank You for a divine strategy, and I believe, therefore I speak, I decree and declare that my words will touch the heart of the King and heal the wounds of the little boy inside, in Jesus' Name.

I want you to embrace your assignment to Speak to the King and Minister to the Boy. You are more than capable. Frustration and failure are not an option, you just need a new strategy and we believe the Holy Spirit will reveal this to you. You are ready for this book because you are thirsty for something more in your relationship. And you're hungry for more, which will give you access to new levels of power and wisdom.

Just dream for one second. What will it look like when the little boy inside the King is healed? The King becomes unstoppable. Use this picture to fuel your motivation when the seeds you sow don't harvest immediately. Learn to celebrate the King for every ounce of forward movement. A King's greatest pleasure is to be honored unconditionally.

As the King receives unconditional honor from those who love him, the little boy loses his influence.

Remember, the King will respond to you appropriately when you touch his heart.

'Beloved, I wish above all things that thou mayest prosper and be in health, even as thy soul prospereth.'

3 John 1:2 KJV

THE GAME PLAN

Reflections from this Chapter

_____
_____
_____
_____
_____
_____
_____
_____
_____

What did you learn?

➢ _____
    _____

➢ _____
    _____

➢ _____
    _____

➢ _____
    _____

What strategy do you need to implement?

➢ _____

_____

➢ _____

_____

➢ _____

_____

➢ _____

_____

What behavioral change do you need to make?

➢ _____

_____

➢ _____

_____

➢ _____

_____

➢ _____

_____

Who do you know that has perfected the behavioral change that you need to make?

➢ _____

_____

➢ _____

_____

➢ _____

_____

➢ _____

_____

Develop a strategy to perfect the behavioral change.

➢ _____

_____

➢ _____

_____

➢ _____

_____

➢ _____

_____

How will you prioritize the behavioral change?

➢ _____

_____

➢ _____

_____

➢ _____

_____

➢ _____

_____

How often will you practice it?

How will you be consistent until you perfect the change?

_____

_____

_____

_____

_____

_____

_____

CHAPTER 5

Moving the Kings Heart

My wife (Monique) and I have taught and trained couples for over 20 years. We started in the basement of our church, The Resurrection Center (formerly Eight Street Baptist Church). We had no idea that those times teaching Marriage Sunday school would birth an unquenchable desire to see couples #SOAR and #WIN in their relationships.

Every woman must know how to move the King's heart. The position that God has placed man in marriage and head of the household is critical to the family's success. I cannot stress this enough, if there is no King in place, there can be no Dominion. Both men and women were given dominion in Genesis Chapter 1. This simply means that without them ruling side by side, there can be no dominion. Where there is no dominion, there will be breaches in the household. These breaches will affect your finances, children, relationships, and purpose.

Statistics reveal that if a man has a relationship with God, the impact of that relationship will affect the entire household. This specifically relates to the women in their lives. If the man doesn't accept his role as King, how can the woman in his life ever be fulfilled? Everything is riding on you, being able to move his heart in the right direction.

You must understand how powerful you are. And that God has given you influential power to move his heart. You just must discover the strategies on how to do it. Every man must be properly studied and analyzed. Most men are predictable and programmable. We will give you a few principles on moving a man's heart. Read this story below on how this gentile woman for Sidon moved the heart of Jesus.

'Then Jesus went out from there and departed to the region of Tyre and Sidon. And behold, a woman of Canaan came from that region and cried out to Him, saying, "Have mercy on me, O Lord, Son of David! My daughter is severely demon-possessed." But He answered her, not a word. And His disciples came and urged Him, saying, "Send her away, for she cries out after us." But He answered and said, "I was not sent except to the lost sheep of the house of Israel." Then she came and worshiped Him, saying, "Lord, help me!" But He answered and said, "It is not good to take the children's bread and throw it to the little dogs." And she said, "Yes, Lord, yet even the little dogs eat the crumbs which fall from their masters' table." Then Jesus answered and said to her, "O woman, great is your faith! Let it be to you as you desire." And her daughter was healed from that very hour.'

Matthew 15:21-28

Inside every King, there is an innate desire to provide for the ones he loves. A King gets pleasure out of providing for his subjects. In other words, every man wants to provide for the ones he loves. **If you can discover what he loves** and help him see that his lack of movement will harm their lives, you will see movement.

Discovery of what he loves is principle #1.

This gentile woman from Sidon touched Jesus' heart. There is always a positive outcome when you touch a person's heart. Jesus loves people. His very purpose was to preach the Kingdom of God. The Kingdom of God came with the power to heal the sick, raise the dead, and cast out demons.

This woman tapped into His very purpose of why He came on the earth. He came to set the captives free. During His delayed response to her, she worshipped Him. When your request is connected to the man's purpose, he will have a programmed response. I know what you're thinking. Some of you are saying, "Dr. Tim, but what if the man doesn't know his purpose." Ladies, it's your assignment to help him see that his movement will have a direct effect on his purpose. His purpose will bring him fulfillment. Jesus closes by saying that her faith brought Him great pleasure.

Principle # 2 is Make sure your motive is pure. No man likes to be manipulated. Many couples are practicing witchcraft and they don't even realize it. We will use our bodies, sex, and our will for hire. This gentile woman walked for miles to have an encounter with Jesus. Her motive is to see her daughter set from an evil spirit. Your motives must be for the good of the family. You want to see the entire household blessed. As Kings walk in purpose, their women are fulfilled.

Principle #3 Eliminate compromise from your walk with God. Every man needs to see a woman that has an uncompromising walk with God. We have talked with countless women who say they are doing everything that they know to do. Even if the man isn't' right with God himself, you must live without compromise. I'm not saying you need to be perfect, but you need to be moving towards perfection.

The Holy Spirit revealed to us that the reason why some women can't move the man's heart is because of compromise. Truth sanctifies. Compromise will never bring about the change you are hoping for. You must become the change you want to see. Just think about what we're saying. When we entered a relationship with Christ, who changed? Well, the answer is simple, we did. Christ never changed whom to meet our needs; we changed to meet His.

Principle #4 Never compromise the things of God to prove your love for Him. This one is similar to the above principle. Principle # 3 is about you and Principle #4 is about what you are willing to do for him. If you must compromise the things of God to prove your love for him, what you have isn't love at all. The God kind of love will never motivate disobedience. If that man requires you to disobey God to prove your love for him, your relationship is destined for failure.

'The king's heart is in the hand of the Lord, Like the rivers of water; He turns it wherever He wishes.'

Proverbs 21:1

THE GAME PLAN

Reflections from this Chapter

_____

_____

_____

_____

_____

_____

_____

_____

What did you learn?

➤ _____

_____

➤ _____

_____

➤ _____

_____

➤ _____

_____

What strategy do you need to implement?

➤ _____

_____

➤ _____

_____

➤ _____

_____

➤ _____

_____

What behavioral change do you need to make?

➤ _____

_____

➤ _____

_____

➤ _____

_____

➤ _____

_____

Who do you know that has perfected the behavioral change that you need to make?

➢ _____

_____

➢ _____

_____

➢ _____

_____

➢ _____

_____

Develop a strategy to perfect the behavioral change.

➢ _____

_____

➢ _____

_____

➢ _____

_____

➢ _____

_____

How will you prioritize the behavioral change?

➤ _____

_____

➤ _____

_____

➤ _____

_____

➤ _____

_____

How often will you practice it?

How will you be consistent until you perfect the change?

_____

_____

_____

_____

_____

_____

_____

CHAPTER 6

What a KING Needs Most

Your response is your; responsibility…Apostle Michael Freeman

We want to dedicate this chapter to our spiritual parents, Drs. Mike and DeeDee Freeman. Their testimony has inspired thousands and has helped us tremulously. While writing this book, I overheard my daughter having a heated conversation with my wife. She uttered Apostle Mike's statement, "Mom, your response is your responsibility." The power of covenant relationships. (train up a child) Proverbs 22:6.

They are designed to drop nuggets of revelation that can change your life if you apply what you hear. From the first time we heard that phrase, We've e been quoting this in my house, to my children and in counseling sessions with other couples. Our daughter learned the phrase from us, and we learned it from Apostle Mike and Dr. Dee Dee. You know you are living right when your children start correcting you with your own words.

While preparing to write this book and this chapter, I thought about my spiritual mother's testimony from the lips of Dr. Dee Dee, Apostle Mike, who was rude, nasty, and a literal fool in the earlier years of their marriage. This leads me to the title of this chapter, "What a King Needs Most." What a king needs most is a God-fearing woman. A God-fearing woman is a woman that will stand on the principles of God even when her husband isn't acting right. For additional reading, I recommend Leslie Vernick's book "How to Act Right; When Your Spouse Acts Wrong."

Dr. Dee Dee faithfully walked out this principle that her response is her responsibility. Simply she unplugged her emotions and did what she was supposed to do. Some of you may be thinking that this is hard to do, or Dr. Tim, you don't know my situation. I get it and I understand. This why I said what a King needs most is a God-fearing woman. A God-fearing woman can access the grace of God through her submission to God. It is the grace of God that gives us the power to do what is necessary. Speaking to the King and Ministering to the Boy will require the power of God. Grace is the power source that gives us the ability to do the supernatural. What we cannot do in our flesh, we can do through the grace of God. When we submit to God, we now have access to his power.

It is nearly impossible to minister to the boy, when you have a disdain for the king.

When you have disdain for a person, you are still emotionally attached. You can't allow your emotions to affect your decisions, and when you respond out of frustration to the boy you see, not the King who's becoming. Your body language and words will reveal the pain of disappointment and frustration. The need for a human connection and fellowship is very real. God created us for relationships, but what do we do when the relationship is the cause of our pain and disappointment? You must get what you need from God until your partner is willing to provide it. This is a very important principle. So I will repeat it one more time. You must get what you need from God until the partner in your relationship is willing to provide it.

'For the unbelieving husband is sanctified by the wife, and the unbelieving wife is sanctified by the husband; otherwise, your children would be unclean, but now they are holy.

I Corinthians 7:14

The above scripture is one of my favorites. This is a power of revelation. As I said previously when you got married to Jesus, who changed? I submit to you; that God doesn't need to change; He is perfect. It is the unbelieving and unsanctified who are sanctified by their connection to God.

Dr. Dee Dee decided to unplug her emotions and we must unplug our emotions. In other words, you can't allow how someone is acting to influence your behavior. Everything you do must be done in Faith. And for your faith to have any power, it must work through love. This is why the Bible is quoted as saying, "Love never fails." The God kind of love isn't a feeling. The God kind of Love isn't a feeling. Now, I repeated that phase because most of us quote that phrase, but many don't know how to walk that out in the natural realm.

Our emotions play no role in our obedience to applying Godly principles. So why are so many couples motivated by their emotions? A God-fearing woman cares more about honoring God than she feels about getting her needs met.

It is not until the Lord becomes your shepherd that all your needs will be eliminated. Many have made Jesus their Savior, but most people never allow Him to become Lord. When He becomes Lord, the Spirit of the Fear of the Lord will come on your life. It is the Fear of the Lord that began to hover over Dr. Dee Dee's life. It is the Spirit of the Fear of the Lord that brought our Pastor to his knees. What a powerful testimony. This has been the source of my strength in my relationships. The power of covenant connections. Get around people with your answer and get away from people who have your problem.

I will close by sharing my testimony. Years ago, while Monique and I struggled in our marriage, I hit a brick wall. Nothing I seemed to do was working. My emotions were all over the place. I got so frustrated that I cried out to God and simply told him I couldn't do it anymore. I came to the end of myself. Now, when I hear couples come to me and say, "Pastor Tim, Lady Mo, I'm done. Our y response is always good; now we can really get to work.

God is the author of relationships, and he establishes the rules of engagement. If you are going to have a successful relationship, you must obey the rules of engagement. We truly believe the application of this principle saved our marriage. So much so that Monique began to write notes to herself on her bathroom mirror; one of the notes said, "Today, I will love my husband." She also began to notice a change in me. I had to unplug my emotions concerning her. Nothing she did would change what I thought about her or alter my actions toward her. I made a decision that I would do what I was supposed to despite my lack of personal fulfillment.

The glory of God showed up because I got out of a place of fear and entered a place of rest. It is not until you learn how to rest on the promises of God that the Glory of God shows up.

'The Lord is my shepherd; I have all that I need.'
Psalms 23:1

THE GAME PLAN

Reflections from this Chapter

_____

_____

_____

_____

_____

_____

_____

_____

What did you learn?

➤ _____

_____

➤ _____

_____

➤ _____

_____

➤ _____

_____

What strategy do you need to implement?

- ➤ _____
  _____
- ➤ _____
  _____
- ➤ _____
  _____
- ➤ _____
  _____

What behavioral change do you need to make?

- ➤ _____
  _____
- ➤ _____
  _____
- ➤ _____
  _____
- ➤ _____
  _____

Who do you know that has perfected the behavioral change that you need to make?

- ➢ _____
  _____
- ➢ _____
  _____
- ➢ _____
  _____
- ➢ _____
  _____

Develop a strategy to perfect the behavioral change.

- ➢ _____
  _____
- ➢ _____
  _____
- ➢ _____
  _____
- ➢ _____
  _____

How will you prioritize the behavioral change?

➢ _____

_____

➢ _____

_____

➢ _____

_____

➢ _____

_____

How often will you practice it?

How will you be consistent until you perfect the change?

_____

_____

_____

_____

_____

_____

_____

CHAPTER 7

Becoming his Biggest Cheerleader

Every boy needs a mother who believes in him, and every King needs to be motivated by the queen in his life. Boys love their mothers because their mothers are the first to touch their souls. Mothers are the first person that a boy reveals their vulnerabilities too. Mothers become the safe space for us boys. Mothers become boys' first cheerleaders.

At 16, I joined the cross-country team in high school. This memory of my mother being my greatest cheerleader is sketched in my subconsciousness. During this particular time in her life, she had no transportation. She would have to travel by bus whenever I had a track meet.

On this day, my track meet was held at Central High School and she had to take two buses to get there. I remember looking for my mother in the stands. The race was about to start, and I still couldn't find her. As I entered the stadium, entering my last lap, I saw my mother standing in the stands shouting my name. Run, Timmy, run! If you have ever run three miles in competition, you understand the feeling the body has when it is exhausted. But hearing the praise of my mother, my whole body receive the strength to finish strong.

We share this story because the impact that a mother's praise has on a little boy's life would be life-changing for me. As a young boy growing up without a father my mother understood that her boy would be a King someday. She refused to allow personal circumstances to prevent her from missing the opportunity to blow wind in her boy's cells. Remember, the boy and the King are the same person. The boy and the King have this one thing in common. They both need a good cheerleader.

'Therefore, we also, since we are surrounded by so great a cloud of witnesses, let us lay aside every weight, and the sin which so easily ensnares us, and let us run with endurance the race that is set before us,'
Hebrews 12:1

We want you to think about this for one second. God created man in His image. This means the very nature of man has been imparted into man's DNA. Your praise will affect the boy and the King in the same way. The following is how our praise affects God:

- ➢ Our Praise ministers to God (Acts 13:2)
- ➢ Our Praise is being intimate with God (Psalm. 22:3)
- ➢ Our Praise is a weapon used against the attacks of the enemy (Judges 6:12)
- ➢ Our Praise gives God pleasure (Revelation. 4:11)

Allow me to elaborate on how praise can insulate the boy and the King from the attacks from the enemy. The boy and King will both have enemies. The number one enemy of the boys and the King's life is his insecurities.

'And the angel of the LORD appeared unto him, and said unto him,

The LORD is with thee, thou mighty man of valour.'

Judges 6:12

Ladies, please read the story of Gideon and Moses. You will find them in Judges Chapters 6 and 7 and Exodus Chapter 3. What you need is a strategy from God, so you can effectively Speak to the King and Minister to the boy. In Judges Chapter 6, the boy manifested in the King's body. Gideon's insecurities are on full display.

When most men are challenged to perform at higher levels, their insecurity will show up, and they will begin to reflect on whom they think they are not or what resources are lacking. God used this strategy with both Gideon and Moses. Read Gideon's response to God.

If you want the King to respond, you must ignore when the boy is talking.

'So he said to Him, "O my Lord, how can I save Israel? Indeed my clan is the weakest in Manasseh, and I am the least in my father's house."

Judges 6:15

God's response to Gideon was simply, "You are a mighty man of valor." He later told Gideon to go in this might.

Praise is one of the believers' supernatural weapons, especially when it is used to encourage the boy and the King. Praise penetrates through our insecurities and motivates us to tap into the grace of God that God has given every man. You must look for opportunities to praise the boy and the King.

If you can't find something to praise the boy or the King about, you have lost your spiritual sight.

God responded to Moses in the same way. Moses was 80 years old when God called him. The boy in Moses started speaking and God ignored him. God's answer to Moses was, "I'm going with you." All of Moses' insecurities left him and the rest was history. Two million people through the hands of Moses.

This is not a one-time event. This is something that you must do in faith. Stay in Faith until that boy begins to act like a King.

If the King doesn't respond to your voice, then minister to the boy.

I pray that a fresh zeal would come on now in the Name of Jesus and the wisdom God would confirm your strategies with miracles, signs, and wonders.

'But thou art holy, O thou that inhabits the praises of Israel.'
Psalm 22:3

THE GAME PLAN

Reflections from this Chapter

_____

_____

_____

_____

_____

_____

_____

_____

_____

What did you learn?

➢ _____

_____

➢ _____

_____

➢ _____

_____

➢ _____

_____

What strategy do you need to implement?

➢ _____

_____

➢ _____

_____

➢ _____

_____

➢ _____

_____

What behavioral change do you need to make?

➢ _____

_____

➢ _____

_____

➢ _____

_____

➢ _____

_____

Who do you know that has perfected the behavioral change that you need to make?

➢ _____

_____

➢ _____

_____

➢ _____

_____

➢ _____

_____

Develop a strategy to perfect the behavioral change.

➢ _____

_____

➢ _____

_____

➢ _____

_____

➢ _____

_____

How will you prioritize your behavioral change?

➢ _____

_____

➢ _____

_____

➢ _____

_____

➢ _____

_____

How often will you practice it?

How will you be consistent until you perfect the change?

_____

_____

_____

_____

_____

_____

_____

CHAPTER 8

Pushing Him to Perfection

In this chapter, we will deal with two topics. Helping the boy see like a King and holding them accountable to becoming a King. I want to say that this will be a difficult assignment, but with God's help, you will prevail. There is one precursor, please keep it in mind. You must get your strategies from God. In other words, get your strategies from the truth. Have you ever noticed that truth is universal? And being used by all successful people. Truth is being used by motivational speakers, business executives, teachers, and all those looking to achieve impactful results.

As believers, we know from the Word of God that truth comes from God. God is the originator of truth, and the truth is absolute. As you search for strategies for Speaking to the King and Ministering to the boy, you will discover that the strategy doesn't have to originate from you. We mentioned before that we must hang with those who have our answers and get away from those who have our problems.

The answers and the strategies you need have already been made available; you must seek them out. The Bible talks about "seek and you shall find" and "knock and the door will be opened." This is not just a Bible principle; this is true in life. Success in any endeavor is not an accident. It is the product of pursuit, thirst, and determination to succeed. If you are going to push him to perfection, you must acquire a dog-like mentality. We use the word dog because there is a character in the Bible called Caleb. In Hebrew, the name Caleb means dog.

Caleb had a dog-like mentality, he believed whatever God said. He was tenacious. If God told Caleb that he could have it, he knew that with God's help, you would prevail. Pushing him to perfection will require you to have a dog trainer mentality. No one receives any amount of success in life without a little pressure. In your pushing, you are simply applying the necessary pressure for forward movement. Strategy number one is 'Helping the boy see like a King.'

A man's ability to see clearly will be the key to their movement. As you are driving, have you noticed that your speed depends on your visibility? We accelerate when visibility is clear, and we decelerate when visibility is impaired.

Helping the boy see like a King will require you to see him through the eyes of his Heavenly Father.

Ladies, you have a big assignment. Turning Potential into Purpose. How do you respond when you realize the man you married is still operating in his boy character? We know you saw purpose, but we are just seeing potential.

The man you fell in love with is in there, but the little boy in him seems to shine more. He may drive a nice shiny big car, but when he pulls up, you see a scooter. You serve him a King's meal, but when he is eating, you see him eating out of a three-compartmentalized tray. How do you change your perception of what you see in the natural?

The first thing is to go to God and ask Him to refresh your memory of what you saw in the beginning. A strong, daring, confident man that can do anything & everything without hesitation. (That is a lot).

'A man that finds a wife finds a good thing and receives favor from the Lord.' Proverbs 18:22

When I was developing my relationship with my mother-in-law, I had to explain to her that I am not taking your son away, I am picking up where you left off. Women must continue to nurture, develop, and assist wherever their last connection stopped.

Sometimes women think that men are fully developed when God will use a woman to take them to the next level and season in life. We often forget that they have already been raised, but we are called to help and nurture them like one of our children. Although they may have proclivities as a child, we must Speak to the King and remind him who he is so they can make mature decisions. That happens because they are not fully developed and it may appear that they are walking but actually crawling. The way you minister to the King when he is acting like a boy is to minister to him with affirmations. Little children like to be rubbed, spoken too softly, and soothed, so you use King's words with motherly touches, so they will feel comforted and not feel reprimanded and manipulated. This will build their confidence in your love for them.

When touching them, make sure your touch is light and soft. When trying to get him to move, be firm but persistent. Be encouraging, uplifting, inspiring, and motivational. Remember how they were raised and spoken to as a child; that will help you to determine how to get the man to turn.

'Finally, my brethren, be strong in the Lord and the power of his might.'

Ephesians 6:10

THE GAME PLAN

Reflections from this Chapter

_____

_____

_____

_____

_____

_____

_____

_____

What did you learn?

➢ _____

_____

➢ _____

_____

➢ _____

_____

➢ _____

_____

What strategy do you need to implement?

➢ _____

_____

➢ _____

_____

➢ _____

_____

➢ _____

_____

What behavioral change do you need to make?

➢ _____

_____

➢ _____

_____

➢ _____

_____

➢ _____

_____

Who do you know that has perfected the behavioral change that you need to make?

➤ _____
_____

➤ _____
_____

➤ _____
_____

➤ _____
_____

Develop a strategy to perfect the behavioral change.

➤ _____
_____

➤ _____
_____

➤ _____
_____

➤ _____
_____

How will you prioritize the behavioral change?

➢ _____

_____

➢ _____

_____

➢ _____

_____

➢ _____

_____

How often will you practice it?

How will you be consistent until you perfect the change?

_____

_____

_____

_____

_____

_____

_____

CHAPTER 9

Speaking Vs. Listening "The Power of Silence"

Everything we see was created by a spoken word. The value you place on your words is revealed through the health of your emotional state. An emotionally unhealthy individual has not learned how to control their tongue. Speaking to the King and Ministering to the boy will require you to value both speaking and silence. The key to knowing when to talk and when to listen is a skill that must be developed.

Becoming a good speaker requires being a good listener. Professional communicators will say that more words are being spoken through our body language than through our lips. We just must become good listeners. Many of us are speaking when we should be listening so that we will know what to say. Knowing how to recognize the voice of the king and the voice of the boy will require you to exercise the power of silence.

We want to introduce a strategy that we believe will yield supernatural results. There are many times that we communicate with our partners, and it seems like they are not listening. What do you do when you are not being heard? Farmers will tell you that when clouds fill up with water, they release rain. Our words are like seeds and when you sow them, you do not always have to sow them again. You just move into a posture of prayer.

As Pastors, we have told our church that we will never pray for money. Money is not just going to fall from the sky. Money comes to us because of sowing seeds. This same strategy can be used in our relationships. Once you have said what needs to be said, simply start praying. Prayer is equivalent to asking God for the rain. It works like faith and patience. Once you release your faith, you must exercise patience. You must pray once you speak to the King and minister to the boy.

You must begin praying for the answer, not the problem. What do you want the King to see, and what do want the boy to understand? Below are some scriptures that I recommend using to decree and declare.

'Ask the Lord for rain In the time of the latter rain. The Lord will make flashing clouds; He will give them showers of rain, Grass in the field for everyone.'

Zechariah 10:1

'Then He said to them, "These are the words which I spoke to you while I was still with you, that all things must be fulfilled which were written in the Law of Moses and the Prophets and the Psalms concerning Me." And He opened their understanding, that they might comprehend the Scriptures.'

Luke 24:44-45

'do not cease to give thanks for you, making mention of you in my prayers: that the God of our Lord Jesus Christ, the Father of glory, may give to you the spirit of wisdom and revelation in the knowledge of Him, the eyes of your understanding being enlightened; that you may know what the hope of His calling is, what are the riches of the glory of His inheritance in the saints,'

Ephesians 1:16-18

'You will also declare a thing, And it will be established for you; So light will shine on your ways.'

Job 22:28

'And Elisha prayed, and said, LORD, I pray thee, open his eyes, that he may see. And the LORD opened the eyes of the young man; and he saw: and, behold, the mountain was full of horses and chariots of fire round about Elisha. '

2 Kings 6:17

Jesus gave us this principle when he said in Matt. 26:41. While you are silent you ought to be steadfast in prayer. The heart of the king is in the hand of the Lord and God has the power to move the heart (Pr. 21:1). You will win this battle with constant prayer. Practice the discipline of silence and allow the Holy Spirit to move.

You do not always have to correct the King, especially if you know the King isn't listening. Your silence will allow the Holy Spirit to work for you. If he makes an unwise decision, he learns to value his voice (especially if you remain silent). If he makes the right decisions, his confidence in himself grows. Either way, you win.

In the book of Genesis chapter 1. God told Adam not to eat the Tree of Good and Evil. During the time of temptation, God remained silent. Have you ever wondered why God was silent? All through the Bible, you will discover that sometimes God remains silent when has already spoken.

God knew that Adam would have made the wrong decision, but in making wrong decisions, growth takes place. There are times when you must allow the man to fail. It is through failure that we become more sensitive to instruction. Pray this prayer with me.

Father in the Name of Jesus, open his eyes that he may see. Enlighten the eyes of his understanding and remove the scales from his heart so that he may hear His voice. Equip me with the words say and rain on every word that I sow into his heart. Allow his heart to receive the engrafted word that can deliver his soul in Jesus' Name.

'Don't use foul or abusive language. Let everything you say be good and helpful so that your words will be an encouragement to those who hear them.'

Ephesians 4:29

THE GAME PLAN

Reflections from this Chapter

_____

_____

_____

_____

_____

_____

_____

_____

What did you learn?

➢ _____

_____

➢ _____

_____

➢ _____

_____

➢ _____

_____

What strategy do you need to implement?

➢ _____

_____

➢ _____

_____

➢ _____

_____

➢ _____

_____

What behavioral change do you need to make?

➢ _____

_____

➢ _____

_____

➢ _____

_____

➢ _____

_____

Who do you know that has perfected the behavioral change that you need to make?

➢ _____

_____

➢ _____

_____

➢ _____

_____

➢ _____

_____

Develop a strategy to perfect the behavioral change.

➢ _____

_____

➢ _____

_____

➢ _____

_____

➢ _____

_____

How will you prioritize the behavioral change?

➤ _____
_____

➤ _____
_____

➤ _____
_____

➤ _____
_____

How often will you practice it?

How will you be consistent until you perfect the change?

_____
_____
_____
_____
_____
_____
_____

CHAPTER 10

Self-Development is the Key

The very nature and the origin of the relationship was established by God. Adam and Eve is the foundation on which God has established the purpose of our relationships. Two separate individuals become one flesh. This process cannot occur without self-development. Self-development must be embraced to have fulfillment. Often, we get distracted by what the other person in the relationship is not providing, but it is our commitment to self-development that gives us access to the Grace of God.

This grace then becomes the power source that provides for the needs of the relationship. At the time of writing this book, we were celebrating 27 years of marriage. It is the years we have spent together that we self-developed and helped us get through disappointment. If couples don't self-develop; the success of their marriage would be in jeopardy. Relationships, by their very nature, require growth.

As you conduct your self-examination, you will discover that it is your relationship that is your curriculum development. As we mentioned earlier when you get into a relationship with Jesus, who changes? The short answer is that you are required to change and mature in the body of Christ. The same is true in your relationship.

It is the relationship that reveals your fleshly deficiencies. You noticed we said fleshly. In your regenerated spirit, there are no deficiencies. You must access what you need from your regenerated spirit. When you realize this, it will snatch you out of self-pity. Many people fail at this process because they are trying to do it in their flesh, which can only be done through the spirit. Look at the below scripture.

Another mistake we see individuals make is losing their focus. They focused on the other person changing instead of focusing on Jesus. Jesus is our measuring stick for our self-development. As we look at Jesus, we see clearly where we must become like him.

'For the flesh lusts against the Spirit, and the Spirit against the flesh; and these are contrary to one another so that you do not do the things that you wish.'

Galatians 5:17

Your relationship demands that you grow. You must ask yourself, what fruit of the Spirit should be coming from my life and flowing into my relationship? What your relationship is lacking is what you need to become. Love will always anticipate need; this is why love never fails.

'But the fruit of the Spirit is love, joy, peace, longsuffering, kindness, goodness, faithfulness, gentleness, self-control. Against such, there is no law.'

Galatians 5:22-23

The fruit of the Spirit will not appear automatically in your life. It will require your obedience to the Word of God.

I want you to never forget what I'm about to say. Selfishness is at the root of all relationship failures. Just reflect on what I'm saying.

Selfishness is the root of the lack of compromise, the lack of giving, the lack of love, the lack of compassion, and the lack of honor.

You cannot claim to be in love if your love is based on conditions. I'll love you if you do that, I'll give you this to you if you give me that.

This happens in relationships all the time. The sad part is that many couples do not even realize that they are practicing witchcraft. You are practicing witchcraft when your love and honor for one another becomes conditional. Witcraft is using your power and influence to control the behavior of another.

There are four things you must do to self-development.

> Identify what you need to become (this is you becoming more Christ-like)
> Humbly surrender to truth (this is the strategy)
> Die to your flesh daily (this defeats selfishness)
> Practice the above until perfect.

As we bring this book to a close, here are a few thoughts to leave with you... Most people don't realize that faith alone will not help you self-develop. It is what you add to your faith that will make the difference. Read the below scripture aloud.

'But also, for this very reason, giving all diligence, add to your faith virtue, to virtue knowledge, to knowledge self-control, to self-control perseverance, to perseverance godliness, to godliness brotherly kindness, and brotherly kindness love. For if these things are yours and abound, you will be neither barren nor unfruitful in the knowledge of our Lord Jesus Christ.'

II Peter 1:5-8

Your relationship will demand everything you got. If Jesus gives His life for us, we must give our life for our relationship. In II Peter, we see you will never stop growing if you continue to add to your faith everything necessary to win. Barrenness is a choice and the refusal to give of yourself is a sign of selfishness. Don't allow the demands that are placed on you to move you into self-preservation. Self-preservation is a fleshly response and surrender is a spiritual response. You will receive the breakthrough desire as you surrender and continue to die daily.

'But we all, with unveiled face, beholding as in a mirror the glory of the Lord, are being transformed into the same image from glory to glory, just as by the Spirit of the Lord.'

II Corinthians 3:18

THE GAME PLAN

Reflections from this Chapter

_____

_____

_____

_____

_____

_____

_____

_____

What did you learn?

➢ _____

_____

➢ _____

_____

➢ _____

_____

➢ _____

_____

What strategy do you need to implement?

➤ _____

➤ _____

➤ _____

➤ _____

What behavioral changes do you need to make?

➤ _____

➤ _____

➤ _____

➤ _____

Who do you know that has perfected the behavioral change that you need to make?

➢ _____

_____

➢ _____

_____

➢ _____

_____

➢ _____

_____

Develop a strategy to perfect the behavioral change.

➢ _____

_____

➢ _____

_____

➢ _____

_____

➢ _____

_____

How will you prioritize behavioral change?

➤ _____

_____

➤ _____

_____

➤ _____

_____

➤ _____

_____

How often will you practice it?

How will you be consistent until you perfect the change?

_____

_____

_____

_____

_____

_____

_____

CHAPTER 11

A MAN NEEDS A MAN CONNECTION A COVENANT–A CONNECTION

Let's close this book by discussing what the root of every King's success will depend on. You've heard it said that behind every good man is a good woman. This is also true when it comes to becoming a Kingmaker. Behind every good King, a King whom he emulates.

'but imitate those who through faith and patience inherit the promises.'
Hebrews 6:12

In the above verse, the concept of modeling is revealed. It's difficult for one to become what one cannot see. It is imperative that if the boy is to become a king, he must sit at the feet of the King. As the woman is his life, you should take personal responsibility in helping your King locate his covenant connections.

This principle has been practiced by all great men, saved or unsaved. This principle goes beyond cultural, religious, and economic status. Every successful man has a story of a covenant connection. What is a covenant connection? A covenant connection is a person that is assigned to your life. It is also a person that you can glean from. A covenant connection may not be a person that you have a personal relationship with. A personal relationship is not necessary for you to get what you need, but you do need access to their information.

Growing up in the inner city of Philadelphia, I learned that whatever you don't have, God will make it available to you through surrogates. You must be able to recognize this convenient connection. I grew up without a father in my home, but three men were placed in my life to take up that vacancy. My beloved uncle, grandfather, and stepfather fulfilled the role of a father in my life.

The spiritual vacancy in my life was fulfilled by Bishop George Williams, the father of my wife, Monique. In my professional career, there was a man named Murray Williams. Everything I needed to know about being black in Corporate America, I learned from Murray Williams. This man would correct my grammar and build my confidence at the same time. He knew how to Speak to a King and Minister to a Boy. He saw the little boy in me and Spoke to the King.

Most men that are struggling in life are struggling because they lack a covenant connection. They also lack accountability and walk in Pride. A man that doesn't understand the value of a covenant connection will struggle to operate at peak levels.

I gave you all that background because I want you to understand that a man will need a covenant connector at every stage and area of his life. We need covenant connection for our marriage, our finances, our business, self-development, fears areas, our ministry, and to parent our children. Some of these roles can be filled by the same individual.

I remember the day I met Bishop S. Todd Townsend. The first time I heard him teach, I knew he was called to be my Pastor. God assigned him to ignite the teaching gift in me. Years later, my wife was responsible for me meeting my next covenant connection. My wife saw what was missing in my life and put me in front of another King. This king is Apostle Mike

Freeman.

Apostle Freeman taught me FAITH. Special thanks to Bishop George Searight and my dear friend Apostle Tony Brazelton. I would have been lost without these great men. I owe them a debt that I cannot pay. They all saw the boy and Spoke to the King.

My loving wife Monique and I chose these great men in my life together. If your King hasn't identified these covenant connectors, you search them out and put them in front of him. You must use all your influence to help him see that he cannot go into it alone. You cannot allow him to be a King unto himself. He must be submitted to a King. Jesus submitted to the Father and a King must be submitted to another King who submits to Christ.

You will discover that:

A man who is not submitted has limited power. That power is limited to himself.

The value of covenant connection is that we gain access to the same anointing we are willing to submit to. It is a beautiful thing. It is a picture of the relationship between God the Father and our Lord Jesus Christ. Jesus valued covenant connection so much so that He said: "I will only do what I see my Father do and I will only say what I hear my Father say." Jesus had access to the Father's power through connection. Your king needs covenant connections. Help him find them. Help him keep them and help him develop them.

SPEAK TO THE KING, MINISTER TO THE BOY

ABOUT THE AUTHORS
Drs Timothy and Monique Johns

The Relationship Dr's Tim and Monique Johns have been married for 27 years. Their transparent approach to providing practical solutions to everyday relationships challenge has inspired thousands. They believe that to be Married for Life (M4Life), both partners must die to their selfish nature. Putting to death selfishness is the number one key to having a successful relationship.

Through their journey together, they have purposely remained friends. Their friendship has produced flexibility and cohesiveness, which has been the other source of their longevity.

Tim & Monique's triangle of LOVE is supported by God being their ex-factor.

They are also the founders of Heaven's Gate Ministries, The Dream Leadership Institute, A Helping Hand, Living Outside the Walls, and several businesses. Their Relationship Drs' broadcast can be viewed weekly on all social media platforms. They are the proud parents of Gabriella, Timothy II, Vincenzia, and Giovanna.

Their scriptural focus: Hebrew 13:5 "For he said himself, I would never leave you or forsake you." M4Life!